Deflower My Flower

Deflower My Flower copyright © by DaVesha Kindred. All rights reserved in the United States of America. No part of *Deflower My Flower* may be reproduced, stored in a retrieval system, or transmitted in any means without written and signed permission from the author except in the case of reprints in the context of reviews.

©2020Kindred

A Bouquet Of Somebodies,

Fantasies,

Romance Me,

Lust For Thee,

Love On She,

She Is Me.

Lily

Your tongue smeared in betwixt my lips,

Stimulating my inner thoughts and outer moans,

Eyes shut so tight igniting my universe oh so right,

Blessing me before you eat your meal,

Savoring every taste,

Clutching my toes inward,

As you swiftly sway your tongue against my neck,

Caressing my ass and making me break a sweat,

Cruising your tongue from my nape to my tail bone,

Sending chills of sublime ecstasy throughout my temple,

Imprinting your name into my soul,

I love how you make me feel so delicate in your arms,

Precious as a field full of lilacs oscillating into the beguiling night,

Still and subtle as your finger massages my ovule,

Sending sensations sprouting supplely about,

Sensually sliding my legs to your head,

Your head to my delightful nutrients,

Supplying you with the eccentric sap,

You begin to disappear as mine eyes shut,

Having an outer body experience as we motion waves,

Mimicking the lilacs and the way they oscillate,

Your body demands control,

I can hear the sounds of the heavens whisper to my inner self,

I stutter words of assurance giving myself fully to you,

Quivering with eruption due to your suction,

The tides are at an extreme high,

I yearn for you to place your flower upon me,

As you deflower my flower,

Gradually making me a part of you,

My limbs growing weak as if my petals are sprouting,

I am whole,

You pin me down and I have come into you,

The stem to your flower,

We are embedded in one another,

You breathe a tune that is music to my core,

Bringing paradise to your conscious,

Sensations to captivate your every intake of my majestic liquid courage,

Releasing your pollen onto me,

Drown me in your sweet honey.

Sunflower

Face up,

You are my Sun,

Shining down on me,

Sending rays of pulsation,

Through the tunnels of my tubes,

Leading the way with every motion,

Vibrations of your adoration making me ooze,

I worship you my Sun,

As you bring your energy onto me,

Allowing me to burst into sounds of fulfillment,

Hitting me with each blow to the back,

Glowing over me,

Sweat dripping as you tower over me,

Thanks to you I now know vulnerability,

I desire the praise you bring to my temple,

And as you go down my Sun,

To prove to me your loyalty,

I give to you my tasty oils,

Healthy for your soul,

Draining me of my own exhaustion,

Sending rays of erections,

I gravitate to the core of your heart,

Feening for the way your mouth grips my body,

Sucking my life into vibrancy,

Wavelengths of moans go into another dimension,

Gone with the wind goes the built-up tension,

A good deed you have done releasing your sweet graces onto the petals of my flower,

Giving me growth,

I am now loyal to you,

Receiving you in droplets,

Nourishing me,

Quenching my thirst,

I am now faithful to you my Sun.

Rose

Wrapped in your arms,

Your petals cover me whirly,

You are so gentle with me,

My thorns are no longer,

As you sing me into the deep tones of your love,

Your soft skin brushes up on me,

Holding me captive my delicate rose,

As I gravitate my tongue in spirals around your bud,

Shivers going down your spine as I romance you deeply in love,

Making love to you claiming your innocence,

Your taste is so pure,

Your scent lingers,

Drawing me in,

I admire the way you unfold with me,

Coiling our bodies into a cycle of gentle fucking,

Leaving my body floating in midair,

Thorns are no longer.

Jasmine

Jasmine sweet Jasmine,

Placing your delicate fingers on my face to bring me closer,

Bringing your face near my neck,

Your tongue gracefully dancing in my field of sweet Jasmine,

I begin to arch my back into hills touching the Sun as my waters nourish you fully,

Using me and I like it,

Your aroma is heavenly,

Luring my lips to your tropical inner thighs,

Vivacious rise of your physical and mental stimulation,

From my majestic powers onto your corolla,

Your slow whimpers gaining color as I insert my sprouts into the depths of your stem,

Euphorically shaking uncontrollably my sweet Jasmine,

Succumbing as I grind sweet nothings into your caves of purity.

Tulips

your curves,

capture me,

infatuations at its all-time high,

as I massage my tongue in between your

two lips,

you feel so moist and soft,

your performance is never off,

none of your waters are left standing,

no shade but the sun is where we landing,

the way your two lips spread is never-ending,

the way you sway your curvy hips,

the smoothness of your lips,

I can't get a grip,

your bellows are ascending,

the feeling of your bulb filling,

quenching my everlasting thirst,

I can feel your waters in me disperse,

your body folds,

and I go like we rehearsed.

Lavender

I give you the upper hand,

I'll let you take the lead,

Give to me fulfillment and plant your seed,

Grow inside of me and make me plead,

I am guilty of our passion,

You making sacred love to me,

The calmness you give my soul,

When you take control,

Your beauty has me captivated,

Your fragrance follows me in my dreams,

I am devoted to your heart,

As you spread my legs apart,

You give me the royal treatment,

Your tongue feels so elegant as it trains her to cry,

These waters will never run dry,

Oh how you make me feel like a woman,

You keep having me coming,

This is our lust story,

Of how you treated my inner body like luxury,

I yearn for you my higher power,

I want to feel your control my sovereign,

Hover over me and sink into my skin,

I can't wait to sync with you again.

Sweet Pea

Our connection gave me an instant erection,

Your soul stimulated my mind,

You kept me guessing,

Longing for your existence,

Reminiscing about your kisses,

I have been aromatized,

Detained by your enchanting eyes,

I've realized I no longer need a disguise,

My delicate muse,

Your ornamental scent plastered upon my face,

As I blissfully pleasure in between your wings,

Your moans are like silk,

We can make an EP with the way you sing,

Tunes so luxurious,

Pure satisfaction is what I'll gift to you since you're curious,

Igniting the depths of your identity,

As I send vibrations to pleasure you into a love spasm,

Parading you with cosmic orgasms,

Intense lovely moments shared between me and you,

For now we depart and bid adieu.

Iris

I admire the silhouettes you've imprinted in my mind,

I summon you my goddess,

You + me = sublime times,

Your uniqueness makes me grow weak,

To have you stretched out is the goal I aim to meet,

I've gained the courage to convey deep sentiments,

Leaving a room full of evidence,

Showing we're making love and it's evident,

Gifting you with the richness of my kisses,

From your head to your toes I'll make you miss this,

Sending out bursts of rainbows,

Energizing your temple making you glow,

Putting in work while I rip off your clothes,

Admiring you while you pleasure yourself,

Using your fingers to fulfill all your holes,

Deeply aroused while you tease my soul,

Aching to feel you plug me slow,

Leading me to the heavens,

You've guided my soul to its resting flow,

My petals fall onto your garden,

An early bloom is arising,

Bodies folding,

Eyes closing,

The way we've cum is tantalizing.

Bird of Paradise

The way you've aroused my soul was unexpected,

An outer body experience is accepted,

You are paradise on Earth I won't reject it,

Your legs straight up in the air while the mirror reflect it,

I'm soaring to your portal while your wings are wide open,

Got your waterfalls running from when I dove in,

I lay my passion into the hands of paradise,

Got to put my tongue where you like and be precise,

Feed to me your medicines and cure me from my pain,

My tongue flicks upon you driving you insane,

As you beautifully bloom and unclench your arms for just a moment,

I slide my fingers inside you while I got you moaning,

Warm while shivering sending glitches down your stem,

I set you free to spread your wings and take flight,

My body on your body is your kryptonite,

Grinding sensations into the depths of your mind,

Legs locked embracing the sensations while you recline,

Exposing to me your erotic submissions,

I pick you up and set you down as we finish in the kitchen.

Lily

Restorations are in the works,

While I put in that work this is your perk,

Devote your soul to me for one night,

I'll extend your legs and make you bloom it's only right,

Your beauty radiates as you open your gates,

You allow me to escape reality,

Syncing your body into my identity,

I gained new personalities,

I've deepened my spirituality,

Admiring the way you praise my body,

Gently caressing my spot,

I'll do you a favor and show you what I was taught,

I'll pin you down and make you plead,

Trib you right and show you what you need,

Leave trails of passion down your spine,

Release your innocence while I stop time,

Your purity will drift away,

While I freak you down like we're on vacay,

Waiting is a waste let's get it on,

For us to make a movie,

So I can see you on the big screen where you belong.

Daffodil

I'd like to have you in two's,

In all your hues,

I'd take you to the garden you choose,

The way you illuminate the sky from the ground,

I'll enlighten you on a subject you can't refuse,

I would like to take you both and keep you close while we play a game,

While one lay down the other stand tall like a crane,

I'll make y'all go insane and ensure I rid you of all your pains,

I crave the natural high you secrete when I taste your name,

And for her it's the same,

The taste of good fortune activates my tongue,

I lick you on every spot that's fun,

I'm intrigued by the way your waters run,

The way I catch you in my mouth and let you scream and shout,

I see that you're the best performer,

She pleasing me while I'm pleasing you,

You've caught my eyes and now I'm stuck in your corner,

I need to see you squirt while you wait for rebirth your honor.

Dahlia

You are all mine,

My beloved as you stand there wrapped in the sheets so fine,

We now put your portal to rest,

The way you've inflicted your pure love on me I must confess,

I am fascinated with the way you say my name,

Shouting into the void like you're at an auction and I'm the prize you claim,

Allow your tears to help me grow,

Plant a garden and give mine eyes a show,

As you create puddles of sacred waters upon the base of my chin,

Releasing your sprinklers as you're giving in,

Your beauty is mesmerizing capturing me you're tantalizing,

Adventurously pursuing my soul as you balance my body's desires,

Committing to my temple as you pray your love language onto me my sire,

Altering positions you now become submissive,

Exploring your nature thoroughly displaying to you my missive,

Showing to you my deep appreciation as I massage my name into your petals,

Endowed with efficient coition creating echoes of sweet rhapsodies,

Emitting your powers onto my fingers whilst you're belching out melodies,

Succeeding on this journey of satisfaction,

Emphasizing your radiance is my main attraction.

Orchid

I dreamt of you,

Your delicacy,

The way you carry yourself is luxury,

Invite me into your realm of virility,

Ignite my core with your exotic love,

As you tower over my being gracefully stripping yourself bare,

Empowering me with your beauty so delicate and rare,

Conveying to me pure affection,

Gently caressing my bosom,

Massaging my neck with your tongue,

Releasing your masculinity as I stroke your tubes,

Accepting the benevolence I've engraved onto the exhibit set before me,

Tasting your elixir gaining power and strength,

Blooming into an array of colors,

Reviving your pulsating love bud into good health,

Admiring your centerpiece,

As it throbs in studders from my remedy of intimacy,

I only wish this would happen between you and me.

Peony

You fill me with your richness,

Full lips of compassion,

Pounding them with kisses,

Our love making is everlasting,

Twelve rounds of blissfulness,

Curing my body sending my soul blasting,

My chest is rapidly jumping as my heart compresses,

Against your breast recasting my thoughts on love,

Infinitely loving you to infinity and beyond,

All the beyonds in the world.

Dandelion

This tension we have is real,

Being body to body is sending me chills,

I've got the power in my hands to heal,

Give to me your body so I can show you how it feels,

First I devour you like a meal,

You create mountains from your head to your heels,

The crashing of your waters is surreal,

Curing your emotions with the outer burst from our motions,

Mother earth creating rivers and oceans,

The way I'm eating got you boasting,

Sliding my hands in your archways just coasting,

Uncovering the gateway to your soul when I enter got you floating,

Your heavy rains got me craving another coating,

Gifting to me your pleasures you're forever goating,

It is dandy how we're lying in the heavens,

Wishfulness shines through my blinds,

As reality seeps into my skin,

You blow me away with your sweet revenge.

Forget Me Not

Vivid memories take me on a cruise,

When it came to you I always paid my dues,

Accusing you of being my love so true,

On the first night I decorated my face with you,

Spelling my name on your petals so you never forget,

I made you tremble when I got your soul soak and wet,

Never let go of what your eyes once set,

Shouting to Venus as I play you in the cassette,

Therapy to my ears,

I keep you on replay,

Memories of our soul ties still leave me full like I'm at a buffet,

Intaking pieces of these flashbacks every day,

Forget me not,

Never let my imprint on you decay.

Camellia

Your layers are delicate,

Your tolerance is no longer vacant,

Unraveling your deepest desires,

As you desire me,

Your lemony scent inspires me,

I see you in my sleep,

Perfection never smelled so sweet,

Adorable how your hair turns to coils that reaches your feet,

Skin filled with a richness you exceed,

I'll love you forever,

You've already planted your seed,

The growth that you've instilled in me is what your actions feed,

Taking your time as I reveal that you're the reason my heart pumps and bleed,

My intensions are to love you deeply and crave you when you're not around,

To passionately love the rhythms of your soul,

That's my favorite sound,

Camellia is what I use to represent your being,

Too bad I'm in love with a one-night fling.

Ascend.

Amaryllis

I would go to war for you and I only know your name,

Determined to make sparks fly,

I want to see my reflection in your eyes,

Staring into my universe as you hover over me,

I crave to be a part of you,

Hoping to be graced by your beauty infinitely,

I need to taste you,

Have a taste of what's inside,

Anonymously,

Loving,

Whom,

I,

Believe,

You,

To,

Be.

Aster

A star in the form of an angel,

Angelic in the way you be,

Patience serve me when I am with you,

Pure in taste,

Pure in love,

I am in love,

Rivers in my eyes as I create a goddess so fair,

One of a kind my wildflower,

I wish upon the star you appear to be,

That the love we make I feel myself cumming for eternity,

Your majestic treasures got me digging you,

Your magical aura got me reneging who is,

Luscious lover,

Where art thou…

Primrose

First,

My delicate,

I honor you,

My sacred bloom,

As our ceremony for our love is reckoning,

You show me,

No one can do this like you,

Do me how you do,

It is you I cannot live without,

You've never gone astray,

Not when we fuck,

Not any given day,

Monumental you are,

Laying on my alter,

Massaging your central spot,

Intensely gazing,

Your moaning face,

I honor you,

My grace,

Expanding your vocal cords,

As you sing me into another realm.

Myrtle

In the future I long for you to be with me,

To see what I see and feel deeply for you as I have,

You are my half,

You whole me full,

You give to me love that developed its own magnetic pull,

You have my heart and I fully blame you,

Amending my soul into its truest form of beauty,

I would hold your hands with me endlessly,

We will meet again my Aphrodite,

With good fortune,

You will hold me fathomlessly.

Hibiscus

To the love I crave,

Your extravagance haunts my mind,

Extraordinarily occupying my heart from my thoughts,

Creeping in loving me deeply,

Teasing me,

Although I created you,

I hope you are true,

The perfection I've created,

My beautiful.

I've lost the reality of love,

My imagination loves me,

In life the love I imagine is free,

Filled with passion and fun,

Freeing myself from this darkness,

I creep to see the Sun,

I can see.

Morning Glory

The bells are arising,

I've awakened to satisfy your every desire,

Our morning fucks takes my journey higher,

Elevating my addiction to you,

Opening wide,

Blooming,

As we ride into the sunrise,

Your twinkling eyes hidden by the setting of your lids,

Bringing your lips in for one last taste,

Lingering forever,

Massaging your nipples as they sit in my mouth for comfort,

Tongue hugging your body one last time,

As we die down we return to our routine…

Honeysuckle

Honey let me suck you until your petals run dry,

Embrace the tenderness I bring,

Never have to be shy,

I accept your love for what you allow me to feel,

Freedom rings as your tubes fill my surface with pure happiness,

Your sweet aroma hypnotizing to my senses,

It follows me in my dreams,

I can taste your kiss with my thoughts of you,

Honey let me suck on your souls until I am infused with the flames of your love,

Attach your being to my divine sanctuary,

I have been led to you my love,

As we were once lovers in our past lives,

My half for eternity and beyond,

Infinitely embracing the tones of your aura,

Molding my heart into the shape of yours,

Healing my past lives as they dissolve,

Honey let me suck you,

Whilst you cling to my universe,

Release.

Violet

My royal highness,

I am in your presence for just one night,

You attract the world with your everlasting beauty,

You've allowed me to fall head over heels,

Stretching your heels to both ends of the bed,

Expanding your body whole,

Balancing on my tongue as I flick away,

Creating harmony amongst the sky and the earth,

Your universe has restored my taste buds,

Quenched my thirst as I take gulps of your heart,

Violet,

You are my truest love,

Enticing as I fall under your spell,

My undivided attention is all yours my Universe,

I belong to you Violet,

Allow me to heal as I massage my soul onto yours,

Grinding our universe into another dimension.

CPSIA information can be obtained
at www.ICGtesting.com
Printed in the USA
BVHW061942260521
608177BV00012B/1518